D0548507

Barbecues

&

Picnics

TREASURE PRESS

First published in Great Britain in 1985 by

Octopus Books Limited

This edition published in 1990 by

Treasure Press

Michelin House

81 Fulham Road

London SW3 6RB

Reprinted 1992

© 1985 Octopus Books Limited

ISBN 1 85051 016 4

Printed in Hong Kong

ACKNOWLEDGEMENTS

The publishers would like to thank the following companies
for their kindness in providing materials and equipment
used in the photography for this book.

David Mellor, 4 Sloane Square, London SW1 & 26 James Street, WC2
General Trading Company, 144 Sloane Street, London SW1
Harrods, Knightsbridge, London SW1
Log Fires, Fulham Road, London SW7
Neal Street East, Neal Street, London WC2

We would also like to thank the following who were concerned in the preparation of the book.

Series Art Director Pedro Prá-Lopez
Editor Nicole Foster
Photographer Fred Mancini with *stylist* Paula Lovell
Food prepared for photography by Joyce Harrison; Dolly Meers

CONTENTS

NOTE

Standard spoon measurements are used in all recipes

1 tablespoon (tbls) = one 15 ml spoon
1 teaspoon (tsp) = one 5 ml spoon
All spoon measures are level

All eggs are sizes 3 or 4 (standard) unless otherwise stated.

For all recipes, quantities are given in both
metric and imperial measures. Follow either set
but not a mixture of both, as they are not interchangeable.

INTRODUCTION

One of the most pleasant ways of entertaining is cooking and eating out of doors. Barbecues and picnics are becoming increasingly popular, from a simple Sunday lunchtime barbecue for the children to an elaborate celebration picnic for a party of friends. In this book we have tried to make as many suggestions for eating outdoors as possible, to cover a variety of occasions and to ensure that you are never stuck for ideas.

BARBECUES

Equipment

A wide range of barbecue equipment is now readily available, from hardware stores, the hardware departments of some high street chemists, and department stores. One of the simplest and cheapest types of barbecue – and a good model to begin with – is the hibachi ('firebox' in Japanese). It consists of a steel or cast-iron base, in which the charcoal is placed, and a double or treble grill, which can usually be adjusted to different heights. It is a low-standing barbecue so needs to be used on a raised surface, but its size makes it readily portable and easy to store.

The brazier type of free-standing barbecue is suitable for more elaborate cooking and for larger numbers. It stands at a convenient height for cooking and most models incorporate a useful shelf for tools and food. The grill surface is circular and quite large, and in many models is adjustable in height. Other refinements available are a windshield, to protect the cooking area, and a spit above the grill operated by hand or by an electric or battery motor.

At the most sophisticated end of the range are kettle barbecues. They are usually spherical or rectangular in shape with a hinged lid which acts as a windbreak when open. When closed, the dome of the lid reflects the heat, just like an oven. The great advantage of a covered barbecue is that it can be used in windy weather, and the food will still cook evenly and quickly. Kettle barbecues are extremely versatile and can be used for grilling, roasting, or even for baking bread.

Another alternative, well worth considering when redesigning a patio area, is to make your own built-in barbecue. Select a site protected from the prevailing wind and keep to a basic design in proportion to the rest of the garden and the numbers you anticipate entertaining. Fix a metal container inside the structure to hold the fuel, and a grill rack (the racks from an old cooker or refrigerator would be suitable). It is a good idea to line the inside of the barbecue with fire bricks.

Charcoal is the most usual barbecue fuel, bought as lumpwood or as preformed briquets. Although dearer, the briquets give a more intense heat and burn for longer.

Useful barbecue accessories include long-handled tools, to keep hands and arms away from the heat, and tongs with which to turn the food. Aluminium foil is useful for barbecue-baked food. The cook will need an oven glove and a protective apron.

Before lighting the barbecue line the fire bowl with foil. This will speed cooking, by reflecting the heat, and will also make the bowl easier to clean. Spread a thin layer of gravel or sand on the foil to catch dripping fat and reduce smoke.

To light the barbecue, heap the charcoal in the centre of the bowl and (if your barbecue has them) open the air vents. Push a firelighter into the charcoal until only half is showing, and light.

Once the charcoal has begun to glow, more can be added. Cooking cannot commence until the charcoal glows red (or in daylight looks white and dusty) – about 30-45 minutes after lighting. Fresh herbs such as rosemary or thyme can be added to the charcoal to create an aromatic smoke; or wood chips can be scattered over the fire to increase the 'smoky' flavour. As the smoke is quite pungent, the barbecue should be placed in a sheltered spot, to avoid smoke blowing about in the wind, and as far from the house as possible.

To control the heat, open or close the air vents and adjust the height of the grill. Concentrate the heat by heaping up the charcoal, or reduce heat by spreading it further apart. If you need more fuel, allow the new charcoal to warm up gradually round the edge of the fire bowl and rake it towards the centre as it heats up. Older children will enjoy learning to operate the barbecue under supervision, but young children should never be allowed to touch it, and toddlers should be kept right away from the barbecue area.

Cooking

Grilling is the most basic form of barbecue cooking. Many foods can be tenderized and improved in flavour by marinating before grilling. The section on *Marinades and sauces* gives a selection of basic marinades as well as sauces and relishes.

Small pieces of meat can be grilled as kebabs on skewers or minced or finely chopped for hamburger-type patties. The *Kebabs and burgers* section gives a number of different suggestions for these barbecue favourites. Long flat skewers with a sharp point are the easiest to turn on the grill and to spear through the food. Brush the food frequently during cooking with either leftover marinade or oil. Try to prevent the fat from dripping on to the hot coals by tilting the grill slightly forward and, if possible, arranging a narrow drip pan in front of the fire. Each recipe gives an approximate cooking time but the time the food takes to cook on the open grill will vary according to weather conditions: the heat from a barbecue is fiercer than that of a conventional grill,

• A sampling of foods for the perfect barbecue

so as a general rule barbecued food will cook more quickly than oven-grilled.

Larger pieces of food – whole fish, steaks, chops, chicken pieces and sausages – can all be grilled on the open barbecue: see the section on *Joints, steaks and chops* for some unusual suggestions. Rub the grid with a little oil before cooking, to prevent the food from sticking. Start to grill with the rack low for a minute or two, so the food is over very hot heat: searing in this way helps to seal in the juices. Then raise the grill to about 10 cm (4 inches) above the coals and complete cooking.

Spit roasting: A rôtisserie attachment will enable you to spit roast whole joints. The *Joints, steaks and chops* section includes recipes for roasts. After skewering the meat on the spit, make sure that it is properly balanced by rotating it in your hands and checking that it turns evenly. Poorly balanced meat will cook unevenly and damage the motor driving the spit.

When spit roasting, arrange the fire so the heat is on either side of the joint rather than directly underneath, where the outside of the meat would char before cooked through. Spit roasting takes longer than grilling and a larger fire is required to maintain heat.

Entertaining

When planning a barbecue party, remember that appetites seem to increase out of doors. Assemble the food in advance, make sure you light the barbecue in good time and that all utensils and equipment are laid out ready.

Choose a selection of foods with robust flavours and provide picnic plates and cups. The host can supervise the cooking or each guest can barbecue his own food.

Part of the pleasure of a barbecue is the variety of accompaniments offered with the food – from mustards and relishes to tasty breads and salads. The *Barbecue accompaniments* section gives recipes for hot barbecued vegetables and salads with a difference, which can be prepared in advance, as well as some ideas for barbecuing fruit for dessert. The section on *Drinks* provides some interesting suggestions.

PICNICS

Picnics can be great fun, especially for children, and a family day out on the beach or in the country is a part of the pleasures of childhood. But picnics can also be more sophisticated and an excellent way of providing refreshment for a gathering of friends at race meetings, cricket matches and open-air concerts or plays.

Cold weather should not be a deterrent and a picnic around a fire can be an occasion to savour, exciting for children and grown-ups alike. Our *Picnic starters* section includes a hot soup, as well as other suggestions for starters for more formal picnics.

If the journey to the picnic spot is long, remember to take a little something to satisfy the children's appetites: packets of nuts and raisins, crisp apples and a drink. And, to keep them occupied, think up some games: I spy, spelling bees and whispers will keep a car load of children content for many miles.

When organizing a picnic, try to make simplicity the key-note. All the equipment you bring will have to be carried, so keep it to a sensible minimum and keep it light. A compact insulated rigid container is much less cumbersome than the traditional picnic hamper, and it will keep all the food cool, including items such as butter, wine and soda water.

Bring a vacuum flask for iced or hot drinks, and transport soup in a wide-necked insulated jug. Plates, cutlery and mugs should, preferably, be unbreakable and lightweight, but they should not be so flimsy that they make eating difficult.

Pack the picnic methodically so that you know where everything is. Rigid, lidded polythene containers are very useful for a variety of foods. Or pack individual containers with a selection of foods – this is particularly sensible if you are not going to have much space to spread everything out. Pack other foods carefully in foil or polythene bags. *Don't forget* plenty of paper napkins,

damp flannels (in a plastic bag), salt and pepper, a corkscrew, a rug to sit on and (just in case) some insect repellent. With the choice of food, too, simplicity is important. Don't try to re-create an elaborate dinner party menu. Wholesome, traditional food – tomatoes, cold roast chicken, slices of cheese, fruit cake or gingerbread, and chilled white wine – all taste extra good in the open air. More complicated dishes will be required for grander occasions but these should still be straightforward to prepare, transport and serve – there are plenty of suggestions in our section on *Savoury dishes and salads*. For a small group provide one main dish with salad accompaniments; for a larger party you will probably need to provide a selection of dishes.

All the picnic suggestions in this book are for food that can be eaten easily with the fingers or just a fork. Picnic food must keep and travel well and not be too fragile or liable to melt – flaky pastry, too-ripe tomatoes or fruit, and chocolate biscuits, for example, are not suitable. Picnic food should also not be too dry or salty. There is nothing worse than a raging thirst once the thermos is empty. Be sure to bring plenty to drink, if possible, to avoid this situation.

The mainstay of the traditional picnic is the sandwich. It is a perfect outdoor food and a picnic that limits itself to a selection of sandwiches with salad and fruit need never be boring. The section on *Sandwiches and rolls* concentrates on giving as many ideas as possible for sandwich breads and fillings, ranging from the everyday to the exotic.

As a dessert treat, bring a large ripe watermelon – it is fun to eat and thirst-quenching too, particularly on hot summer days.

● A variety of mouth-watering dishes for a picnic

8

Wine marinade

Makes about 300 ml (½ pint)

150 ml (¼ pint) red wine
2 tbls lemon juice
1 onion, sliced
1 carrot, sliced
1 celery stalk, chopped
1 parsley sprig or ½ tsp dried parsley
1 thyme sprig or ½ tsp dried thyme
1 bay leaf
6 black peppercorns, lightly crushed
3 tbls vegetable oil (see recipe)

● Left: Wine marinade; Centre: Herb marinade; Right: Barbecue sauce

Combine all the ingredients in a large bowl and leave to stand for about 1 hour before adding the food. (Add the oil only if the marinade is to be used for lean meat such as chicken, turkey or venison.)

Marinate poultry for 2-4 hours, beef or lamb for kebabs for 1-2 hours, large joints for up to 12 hours in the refrigerator. Turn the food several times during marinating.

Use the excess marinade to baste the food during cooking.

Variations: White wine may be substituted for red to marinate veal, pork, poultry or fish. Add some minced garlic to the marinade for extra flavour.

Herb marinade

Makes about 150 ml (¼ pint)

4 tbls vegetable oil
2 tbls lemon juice
½ tsp dried marjoram
½ tsp dried thyme
salt and pepper
1 garlic clove, crushed
1 onion, finely chopped
2 tbls chopped fresh parsley

Combine all the ingredients in a bowl or place in a screw-top jar and shake well. Adjust the seasoning to taste.

Use the marinade for lamb chops, skewered lamb, chicken and turkey pieces, marinating for 2-4 hours in the refrigerator, depending on the size of the pieces, and turning from time to time.

Variation: When available, use a mixture of fresh chopped herbs instead of the dried marjoram and thyme. Fresh marjoram, thyme, mint, savory and a little rosemary would all be suitable. The total quantity of fresh herbs should be about 2 tsp.

Barbecue sauce

SERVES 4-6

50 g (2 oz) margarine or butter
1 large onion, chopped
2 tsp tomato purée
2 tbls wine vinegar
1 tbls lemon juice
2 tbls demerara sugar
2 tsp English mustard powder
2 tbls Worcestershire sauce
1 tsp clear honey
pinch of mixed dried herbs
1 tsp chilli seasoning
150 ml (¼ pint) water

Melt the margarine in a saucepan, add the onion and fry gently for 5 minutes until soft. Raise the heat a little, add all the other ingredients and stir well.

Bring the sauce to the boil, then reduce the heat and simmer for about 10 minutes until well combined and syrupy. Serve immediately.

Serving ideas: This sauce can be made in advance then reheated in a pan over the barbecue. Serve with chicken, sausages, hamburgers and spare ribs.
Variation: Use chicken stock instead of water.

Mexican chilli sauce

SERVES 4-6

2 tbls vegetable oil
1 large onion, finely chopped
1 green pepper, cored, seeded and
*   finely chopped*
397 g (14 oz) can tomatoes
198 g (7 oz) can red pimientos,
*   drained and chopped*
1 tsp sugar
large pinch of English mustard powder
pinch of chilli powder
1 tbls lemon juice
salt and pepper
1 tbls chopped fresh parsley

Heat the oil in a saucepan and add the onion and green pepper. Fry gently for 5 minutes until the onion is soft and lightly coloured.

Add the tomatoes with their juice, breaking them down with a wooden spoon, the pimientos, sugar, mustard powder, chilli powder, lemon juice and salt and pepper to taste. Stir well and bring to the boil.

Simmer gently for 20 minutes until the vegetables are tender and the ingredients are well combined.

Stir in the parsley just before serving.

Serving ideas: Serve with fish or chicken pieces.
Variations: For a milder sauce, omit the chilli powder and add 1 tsp Worcestershire sauce.

Add minced garlic to the sauce for added flavour.

● Mexican chilli sauce; Tomato barbecue sauce

Tomato barbecue sauce

SERVES 4

1 tbls red wine vinegar
1½ tbls soft light brown sugar
1½ tsp prepared English mustard
salt and pepper
large pinch of cayenne pepper
large pinch of grated lemon rind
1 tsp lemon juice
1 small onion, finely chopped
25 g (1 oz) margarine or butter
4 tbls tomato ketchup
1 tbls Worcestershire sauce

4 tbls water
8 stuffed olives, chopped

Place all the ingredients except the olives in a small saucepan and bring slowly to the boil. Cover and simmer gently for about 15 minutes, stirring from time to time, until reduced and well combined. Stir in the olives.

This sauce will keep several days in a covered container in the refrigerator

Serving ideas: Serve either hot or cold with any barbecued meats.
Variation: Halve the quantity of tomato ketchup and add 2 tbls bottled fruit sauce.

Mint chutney

SERVES 4

2 spring onions, chopped
2 tbls chopped fresh mint
½ tsp salt
1 tsp sugar
1 small green chilli, seeded and
  chopped, or large pinch of chilli
  powder
large pinch of garam masala
1 tbls lemon juice
2 tbls natural yoghurt

Place all the ingredients in a blender
and reduce to a purée. Taste the mixture and add more salt or sugar if necessary. This Indian-style chutney is best
served fresh but it may be kept for up to
2 days in the refrigerator if you wish.

Corn relish

Makes about 1 kg (2 lb)

600 ml (1 pint) white wine vinegar
75 g (3 oz) sugar
1 tbls mustard seed or 1 tsp English
  mustard powder
1 tsp salt
450 g (1 lb) sweetcorn kernels, fresh or
  frozen
1 green pepper, cored, seeded and
  finely chopped
1 red pepper, cored, seeded and finely
  chopped
1 onion, finely chopped
4 celery stalks, finely sliced

In a large bowl, mix a little of the vinegar
with the sugar, mustard and salt to
make a smooth paste, then stir in the
remaining vinegar.

Pour the mixture into a large saucepan and bring slowly to the boil. Add the
vegetables to the pan and simmer, uncovered, for 20 minutes or until the
vegetables are just tender.

Pour into clean, warm jars or bottles
and seal with a vinegar-proof cover.
Label and store.

Serving ideas: Serve with hamburgers, barbecued chicken joints or
barbecued spare ribs.
Variations: For a hotter flavour, use 1
red chilli, seeded and chopped, instead
of the red pepper. For a different taste,
substitute cider vinegar for the white
wine vinegar.

Hamburger tomato relish

Makes about 1.5 kg (3 lb)

1 kg (2 lb) tomatoes, skinned and
  quartered
1 kg (2 lb) red peppers, cored, seeded
  and finely chopped
450 g (1 lb) onions, chopped
2 red chillies, very finely chopped
450 ml (¾ pint) red wine vinegar
175 g (6 oz) soft light brown sugar
4 tbls mustard seed
2 tbls celery seed
2 tbls paprika
2 tsp salt
2 tsp freshly ground black pepper

Place all the ingredients in a large
saucepan and bring slowly to the boil.
Simmer, uncovered, for about 30 minutes until most of the liquid has evaporated to give a thick, pulpy consistency.
Stir frequently as the relish thickens.

Pour into clean warm jars or bottles.
Seal with a vinegar-proof cover, label
and store.

Serving ideas: This relish can be used
to enhance the flavour of hamburgers
and sausages.
Variations: Add 100 g (4 oz) raisins to
the other ingredients. Add chopped
fresh ginger for a piquant variation.

● Top: Hamburger tomato relish;
Centre: Mint chutney;
Bottom: Corn relish

Lamb kebabs with mint

SERVES 4

750 g (1½ lb) boned leg of lamb,
trimmed and cut into 2.5 cm (1 inch)
cubes
½ onion, finely sliced
1 garlic clove, crushed
2 tbls chopped fresh mint
1 tsp chopped fresh parsley
4 tbls olive oil
4 tbls red wine
2 corn cobs, husks and silk removed
mint sprigs, to garnish

Place the lamb, onion and garlic in a large shallow bowl. Add the herbs, oil and wine and stir well to mix. Cover and leave to marinate in the refrigerator for 4-6 hours or overnight, turning the meat once or twice.

Slice the corn cobs crossways into 2.5 cm (1 inch) pieces.

Lift the lamb from the marinade and thread loosely on to oiled kebab skewers alternately with the corn. Reserve the marinade. Cook on a hot barbecue, turning frequently and brushing with the reserved marinade, for 10-15 minutes or until tender.

Serve garnished with mint sprigs.

Serving idea: Serve with a rice salad.

Lamb and mushroom kebabs

SERVES 4

1 onion, chopped
1 garlic clove, crushed
2 tsp dried mixed herbs
4 tbls vegetable oil
6 tbls red wine
1 tbls lemon juice
salt and pepper
750 g (1½ lb) boned leg of lamb,
    trimmed and cut into 2.5 cm (1 inch)
    cubes
8 streaky bacon rashers, rinded
16 mushrooms

Place the onion, garlic, herbs, oil, wine, lemon juice and salt and pepper to taste in a bowl and mix well. Add the lamb cubes and stir to coat. Cover and leave to marinate in the refrigerator for 4-6 hours or overnight, turning the lamb once or twice.

Lift the lamb from the bowl and reserve the marinade. Roll up the bacon rashers. Thread the lamb, bacon rolls and mushrooms on to 4 oiled skewers and brush with the reserved marinade.

Cook on a hot barbecue, turning and brushing once or twice with the marinade, for 10-15 minutes or until the lamb is tender.

Serving idea: Serve with a Three bean salad (see page 38).
Variations: Substitute green pepper pieces, marinated with the lamb, for mushrooms. Place a halved tomato on the end of each skewer for the last 5 minutes of cooking time.

• Lamb kebabs with mint; Lamb and mushroom kebabs

● Top: Tandoori-style beef kebabs; Bottom: Greek kebabs

Tandoori-style beef kebabs

SERVES 4

450 g (1 lb) lean minced beef
1 garlic clove, crushed
2.5 cm (1 inch) piece fresh ginger root,
    peeled and chopped
1 tsp paprika
1 tbls tandoori mixture
½ tsp ground coriander
pinch of chilli powder
salt and pepper
1 egg, beaten
1½ tbls lemon juice
For the yoghurt sauce
150 g (5.29 oz) carton natural yoghurt
3-4 fresh mint leaves, chopped
¼ tsp clear honey
1 garlic clove, crushed
½ tsp ground coriander or 1 tsp
    chopped fresh coriander leaves
1 tbls sunflower oil
pinch of chilli powder
½ tsp paprika
To garnish
fresh chopped coriander leaves or
    parsley
lemon wedges

Place the minced beef in a large bowl. Add the garlic, ginger, half the paprika, the tandoori mixture, coriander, chilli powder and salt and pepper. Mix well and work in the beaten egg to bind. Set aside for 5 minutes.

Divide the mixture into 8 portions and mould into 2 long thin sausage shapes on each of 4 oiled kebab skewers.

To make the yoghurt sauce, combine all the ingredients except the paprika in a small serving bowl, then sprinkle the paprika over the top.

Cook the kebabs on a hot barbecue, turning them frequently, for 10-15 minutes or until browned and cooked through. Sprinkle with the lemon juice and the remaining paprika.

Serve garnished with coriander or parsley and lemon wedges, and hand the yoghurt sauce separately.

Serving idea: Serve with rice and a mixed salad.
Variation: Powdered tandoori mixture is available from Asian shops and some supermarkets. If it is unobtainable, substitute 1 tsp each of ground cumin, turmeric and cinnamon, thoroughly combined.

Greek kebabs

SERVES 4

4 tbls vegetable oil
2 tbls white wine vinegar
2 tbls lemon juice
1 garlic clove, crushed
1 small onion, finely chopped
salt and pepper
1.25 kg (2½ lb) fillet end of leg of lamb,
    boned, trimmed and cut into 2.5 cm
    (1 inch) cubes
2 onions, divided into leaves and cut
    into 2.5 cm (1 inch) squares
8 bay leaves
To garnish
lemon wedges
parsley sprigs (optional)

Place the oil in a large shallow bowl with the vinegar, lemon juice, garlic, chopped onion and salt and pepper. Add the lamb, stir to coat, cover and leave to marinate in the refrigerator for at least 2 hours, turning several times so the cubes remain coated.

Blanch the onion pieces for 1 minute in boiling water, then drain. Lift the lamb cubes from the marinade, reserving the marinade, then thread alternately with the bay leaves and onion pieces on to 4 oiled kebab skewers.

Cook on a hot barbecue, turning and basting with the reserved marinade, for 10-15 minutes or until tender.

Serve garnished with lemon wedges, bay leaves and parsley, if using.

Serving ideas: Serve with a Greek salad (see page 40), hot pitta bread and a bowl of green olives.
Variation: Add 1 tsp ground coriander to the marinade.

Vegetable kebabs

SERVES 4

225 g (8 oz) aubergine, cut into 2.5 cm
  (1 inch) cubes
225 g (8 oz) courgettes, cut into 2.5 cm
  (1 inch) slices
salt
100 g (4 oz) button mushrooms
1 small green pepper, cored, seeded
  and cut into 2.5 cm (1 inch) squares
1 small red pepper, cored, seeded and
  cut into 2.5 cm (1 inch) squares
2 small tomatoes, halved
barbecue sauce (see page 11)

Place the aubergine and courgettes in a colander set over a plate. Sprinkle with salt and leave to stand for about 30 minutes to remove the bitter juices. Rinse under cold running water, then pat dry with absorbent paper.

Steam the aubergine, courgettes, mushrooms and peppers for 5 minutes or blanch them for 3 minutes in boiling water, then drain.

Allow the vegetables to cool slightly, then thread them on to 4 oiled kebab skewers. Pour the barbecue sauce into a shallow dish and lay the kebabs in it. Spoon the sauce over them and leave for 5 minutes.

Lift the kebabs from the sauce and cook on a hot barbecue for 5 minutes. Place half a tomato on the end of each skewer, then turn the kebabs, brush with the barbecue sauce and cook for a further 5 minutes or until the vegetables are tender.

Heat the remaining barbecue sauce in a pan on the barbecue grill and serve separately.

Serving ideas: Serve with jacket potatoes and a Three bean salad (see page 38), for a vegetarian barbecue, or as an accompaniment to meat kebabs.
Variations: Omit the peppers and mushrooms and use cubes of fresh or canned pineapple, firm apricots or peaches instead.

● Left: Vegetable kebabs; Right: Pork and pineapple kebabs

Pork and pineapple kebabs

SERVES 4

*500g (1¼ lb) pork fillet, cut into 2.5 cm
     (1 inch) cubes*
*1 green pepper, cored, seeded and cut
     into 2.5 cm (1 inch) squares*
*200g (7 oz) can pineapple chunks,
     drained*
4 small tomatoes
For the marinade
4 tbls dark soy sauce
2 tbls clear honey
4 tbls medium sherry
1 tsp ground cinnamon
large pinch of pepper
½ tsp ground cloves
4 tbls cold tea
1 garlic clove, crushed

To make the marinade, combine all the ingredients in a large shallow bowl. Add the pork, green pepper and pineapple and turn to coat. Cover and leave to marinate in the refrigerator for at least 2 hours.

Drain, reserving the marinade, then thread the pork, green pepper and pineapple alternately on to 4 oiled kebab skewers, leaving space at the end of each.

Cook on a hot barbecue, turning occasionally and brushing with the marinade from time to time, for 15 minutes. Place the tomatoes on the ends of the skewers and cook for a further 5 minutes, until the pork is tender.

Serving ideas: Serve with Cream cheese stuffed potatoes (see page 35) and a green salad.
Variation: Use 1 tsp ground ginger instead of the cinnamon in the marinade.

21

Deep sea skewers

SERVES 4

4 streaky bacon rashers, rinded
2 cod or halibut steaks, skinned and
   quartered
salt and pepper
8 large cooked prawns, peeled
4 mushrooms
4 tomatoes, halved
watercress sprigs, to garnish
For the marinade
6 tbls lemon juice
salt and pepper
large pinch of paprika
2 tbls vegetable oil
1 bay leaf
1 parsley sprig
1 small onion, sliced

To make the marinade, combine all the ingredients with salt and pepper to taste in a large shallow bowl.

Lay the bacon rashers on a board and stretch them with the back of a knife, then cut in half crossways. Season the fish pieces, then roll each piece in a piece of bacon and place in the marinade. Add the prawns and mushrooms and turn carefully to coat. Cover and leave to marinate in the refrigerator, turning from time to time, for about 4 hours.

Drain, reserving the marinade. Thread fish rolls, prawns and mushrooms on to 4 oiled kebab skewers with the halved tomatoes, alternating the ingredients. Brush well with the reserved marinade.

Cook on a hot barbecue, turning from time to time, and basting with marinade, for about 10 minutes or until tender.

Serve garnished with watercress sprigs.

Serving ideas: Serve with a Courgette, pepper and tomato salad (see page 56) and warm crusty rolls or hot garlic bread.
Variation: For a special occasion, use 8 to 10 large scallops instead of the fish steaks.

Brunch skewers

SERVES 4

175 g (6 oz) streaky bacon rashers,
   rinded
4 small tomatoes
16 cocktail sausages
4 lambs' kidneys, skinned, halved
   and cored
2 tbls vegetable oil
salt and pepper
watercress sprigs, to garnish

Lay the bacon rashers on a board and stretch them with the back of a knife. Cut in half crossways and roll up.

Slice the tomatoes in half; thread one half onto each skewer to begin.

Thread the bacon rolls and sausages alternately with the kidney halves on to 4 oiled kebab skewers. Finish each skewer with a half of a tomato.

Brush the skewered meats with oil, season to taste with salt and pepper, and cook on a hot barbecue for 10 minutes, turning once, or until well browned and cooked through. Garnish the skewers with sprigs of watercress.

Serving ideas: Serve with scrambled eggs as an accompanying dish for a hearty breakfast treat. Serve with warm wholemeal or pumpernickel rolls and butter for a tempting supper dish.
Variations: Add whole button mushrooms to the skewers along with the other ingredients. Substitute 2.5 cm (1 inch) cubes of pork fillet or gammon steak for the bacon rashers. Add slices of green pepper between the pieces of meat for extra colour. Marinate the meat in a mixture of soy sauce and clear honey for a specially tasty flavour.

Top: Deep sea skewers;
Bottom: Brunch skewers

Tangy beefburgers

SERVES 4

50g (2oz) fresh white breadcrumbs
3 tbls milk
450g (1 lb) finely minced beef
1 onion, finely chopped
½ tsp dried basil
½ tsp finely grated lemon rind
25g (1 oz) Cheddar cheese, grated
salt and pepper
vegetable oil

Place the breadcrumbs in a large bowl, pour over the milk and leave to soak for 5 minutes.

Stir in the minced beef, onion, basil, lemon rind, cheese and salt and pepper to taste. Process in an electric mixer or food processor until smooth.

Using floured hands, divide the mixture into 8 equal portions, knead lightly and shape into burgers. Cover and refrigerate for up to 12 hours until ready to cook.

Brush the beefburgers with oil and cook on a hot barbecue for 5 minutes. Turn, brush again with oil and cook for a further 5-8 minutes, or until the beefburgers are cooked according to taste.

Serving ideas: Serve in hamburger buns topped with ketchup, green relish or Corn relish (see page 14).
Variation: Use ½ tsp cinnamon instead of basil.

Bacon franks

SERVES 6-8

4 lean rashers back bacon, rinded
410g (14½oz) can hot dog sausages, drained
For the sauce
6 tbls bottled tomato ketchup
2 tbls French mustard
2 small onions, grated

Halve each bacon rasher lengthways. Wrap a piece of bacon around each sausage and secure firmly with wooden cocktail sticks.

To make the sauce, combine the tomato ketchup, mustard and grated onions.

Place the bacon-wrapped sausages on a hot barbecue and cook for 2-3 minutes, then brush a little of the sauce over each one. Cook, turning and brushing with more sauce, for a further 5-8 minutes or until golden brown on all sides.

Serve with the remaining sauce.

Serving ideas: Serve with finger rolls, Corn relish (see page 14) and Red cabbage and pineapple coleslaw (see page 37).
Variation: For a hot flavour, add a few drops of Tabasco to the sauce ingredients.

Italian-style cheeseburgers

SERVES 4

450 g (1 lb) lean minced beef
1 onion, finely grated
1 garlic clove, crushed
1 tbls tomato purée
1/2 tsp dried oregano
salt and pepper
vegetable oil
75 g (3 oz) Mozzarella cheese, cut into
 4 equal slices
4 tomato slices

Place the beef, onion, garlic, tomato purée, oregano and salt and pepper in a large bowl and stir well to mix. Using floured hands, divide into 4 equal portions and shape into patties. Cover and leave in the refrigerator for up to 12 hours until ready to cook.

Brush the burgers all over with oil and cook on a hot barbecue for 5 minutes. Turn, and after a few minutes place a slice of cheese on top of each.

Cook for a further 8 minutes or until the cheese is melted and the hamburger is cooked according to taste. Top each burger with a tomato slice before serving.

Serving idea: Serve in hamburger buns with tomato relish and a green salad.
Variation: Use 4 slices of Cheddar cheese instead of the Mozzarella.

• Tangy beefburgers; Italian-style cheeseburgers; Bacon franks

Barbecued leg of lamb

SERVES 4-6

2 tbls vegetable oil
2 tbls white wine
salt and pepper
1.5-1.75 kg (3-4 lb) leg of lamb
2 garlic cloves, cut into slivers
10 rosemary sprigs
rosemary sprigs, to garnish

Combine the oil, wine and salt and pepper to taste and brush a little over the lamb. Using a small sharp knife, make slits in the lamb skin and insert the garlic slivers and rosemary sprigs into the slits.

Put the lamb in a polythene bag with the remaining oil and wine mixture. Turn to coat, then leave to marinate in the refrigerator for 2-4 hours, turning from time to time.

Remove the lamb from the bag, reserving the marinade. Insert a rôtisserie spit carefully into the lamb, distributing the weight evenly. Make sure the meat is balanced by rotating the spit in your hands.

Scatter a few sprigs of rosemary on the fire for extra flavour. Cook the lamb over a hot barbecue for 1½-2 hours, basting frequently with the reserved marinade, until the meat is tender but still slightly pink in the centre. Cook for a little longer if well-done lamb is preferred.

Serve carved into thick slices, garnished with rosemary sprigs.

Serving ideas: Serve with a Greek salad (see page 40) or a Cucumber and mint salad (see page 59).
Variation: For spicy barbecued lamb, add 2 tsp ground cumin and 1 tbls paprika to the marinade. Omit the rosemary sprigs.

Barbecued roast beef

SERVES 6-8

1.5-1.75 kg (3-4 lb) sirloin of beef,
  rolled and tied
3 tbls olive oil
1 tbls lemon juice
3 large onions, sliced
melted butter, for basting
1 tbls plain flour
salt and pepper

Rub the beef with the olive oil and sprinkle with the lemon juice. Place half the onion slices in a dish, put the beef on top and cover with the remaining onion slices. Leave to stand for at least 3 hours. Discard the onions or reserve and serve, fried, with the roast beef.

Insert the spit into the beef and roast over a hot barbecue. Place a drip pan beneath the spit to catch the meat juices and baste frequently with melted butter.

After about 20 minutes, when the beef is well browned, dust it with the flour. Allow the flour to dry to a crust, then baste again. Roast the beef for a further 1¼ hours, basting from time to time, until the meat is tender and done according to taste. Season with salt and pepper.

To serve, remove the string and carve the beef into thin slices. Skim the fat from the juices in the drip pan and pour the juices over the beef.

Serving ideas: Serve with jacket potatoes, horseradish sauce and baked courgettes or a green salad.
Variation: Add 1 tsp mustard powder to the flour before dusting the beef.

● Top: Barbecued leg of lamb;
Bottom: Barbecued roast beef

Barbecued lemon chicken

SERVES 4

1.5 kg (3¹/₂ lb) chicken
2 tbls lemon juice
salt and pepper
1 bunch of mixed fresh herbs (such as
*   parsley, thyme, marjoram, chervil)*
shredded lettuce leaves, to serve
herb sprigs, to garnish (optional)
For the sauce
25 g (1 oz) margarine or butter
1 onion, finely chopped
1 garlic clove, crushed
2 tbls red wine vinegar
150 ml (¹/₄ pint) chicken stock
1 tbls prepared English mustard
2 tbls demerara sugar
pinch of cayenne pepper
2 lemon slices
1 bay leaf
2 tbls Worcestershire sauce
6 tbls tomato ketchup
2 tbls tomato purée
salt and pepper

To make the sauce, melt the margarine or butter in a saucepan, add the onion and garlic and fry gently for 5 minutes until soft and lightly coloured. Stir in the red wine vinegar, chicken stock, mustard, sugar and cayenne pepper, and add lemon slices and bay leaf.

Bring slowly to the boil, then simmer for 15 minutes. Stir in the remaining ingredients with salt and pepper to taste. Simmer for a further 5-10 minutes, then discard the lemon slices and bay leaf.

Wipe the chicken and sprinkle the inside with the lemon juice. Season well with salt and pepper inside and out and place the bunch of herbs in the body cavity.

Insert the rôtisserie spit carefully into the chicken, distributing the weight evenly. Make sure the chicken is balanced by rotating the spit in your hands. Brush the chicken with the sauce and cook over a hot barbecue for 1-1½ hours until the meat is tender and crisp and brown on the outside.

Carve the chicken into portions and arrange on a bed of shredded lettuce leaves. Garnish the chicken with a variety of fresh herbs if desired. Heat the remaining sauce and serve it with the chicken.

Serving ideas: Serve with sweetcorn sprinkled with paprika or Baked corn on the cob (see page 34) and Potato salad (see page 38).
Variation: Instead of a mixture of herbs, place chopped fresh tarragon mixed with butter in the chicken cavity, and omit the lemon juice. Baste the chicken with a mixture of chopped fresh tarragon and melted butter instead of the sauce.

● Left: Baked stuffed mackerel;
Right: Barbecued lemon chicken

Baked stuffed mackerel

SERVES 4

4 medium mackerel, cleaned and
    heads removed
2 tbls lemon juice
For the stuffing
25 g (1 oz) margarine or butter
2 cooking apples, peeled and diced
4 celery stalks, diced
50 g (2 oz) sultanas
25 g (1 oz) fresh white breadcrumbs
salt and pepper

To make the stuffing, melt the margarine in a large frying pan, add the apple and celery and fry gently for about 5 minutes until softened. Place in a bowl with the remaining stuffing ingredients and stir well to mix.

Rinse the fish in cold water and pat dry with absorbent kitchen paper. Sprinkle the insides with the lemon juice, and season with salt and pepper.

Spoon a quarter of the stuffing mixture into each fish. Wrap each stuffed mackerel loosely in a large piece of foil. Twist the edges and ends of the foil together firmly to prevent juices escaping.

Place the mackerel parcels on a hot barbecue and cook for about 20 minutes until the mackerel is cooked through. Serve straight from the foil.

Serving ideas: Serve with French bread and baked courgettes.
Variation: Try an orange and walnut stuffing instead of apple and celery: mix together 4 small peeled and chopped oranges, 50 g (2 oz) chopped walnuts and 25 g (1 oz) fresh white breadcrumbs.

Devilled steaks

SERVES 4

4 rump steaks, each about 175 g
  (6 oz), trimmed
pepper
4 tsp French mustard
4 tbls soft light brown sugar
salt
parsley sprigs, to garnish (optional)

Season the steaks with pepper. Combine the mustard and sugar and spread half the mixture over one side of each steak.

Place the steaks on a hot barbecue and cook for 5 minutes. Turn over and spread with the remaining mustard mixture. Cook for a further 5 minutes or until the steaks are cooked according to taste. Season with salt, to taste.

Serve garnished with parsley sprigs if using.

Serving idea: Serve with a mushroom and tomato salad sprinkled with chopped basil and Cream cheese stuffed potatoes (see page 35).
Variation: Substitute 1 tsp Worcestershire sauce for 1 tsp of the mustard.

● Devilled steaks; Carpet bag steak;
Barbecued chicken pieces

Carpet bag steak

SERVES 4

1 kg (2 lb) piece rump steak
225 g (8 oz) can oysters in brine,
  drained
2 tbls lemon juice
freshly ground black pepper
3 tbls vegetable oil
salt
To garnish
2 tbls chopped fresh parsley (optional)
lemon wedges

Slit steak horizontally, leaving one long edge uncut, so it can be opened out like a book. Place oysters on one cut surface of the meat and sprinkle with the lemon juice. Cover with the other half of the steak, then sew up the three cut sides, using a trussing needle and fine string.

Season the steak with pepper and brush with the oil. Cook on a very hot barbecue for 2 minutes on each side, then adjust the height of the grill and cook for a further 15-20 minutes over a low heat or until the steak is cooked according to taste. Season the steak with salt.

Remove the string and cut the steak crossways into 4 slices. Serve garnished with lemon wedges and chopped parsley if used.

Serving idea: Serve with jacket potatoes and a green salad.
Variation: Use a 225 g (8 oz) can of mussels instead of oysters.

Barbecued chicken pieces

SERVES 4

4 chicken quarters
salt and pepper
3 tbls vegetable oil
herb sprigs, such as rosemary, thyme,
  sage, mint, to garnish
For the marinade
1 onion, chopped
1 garlic clove, crushed
4 tbls tomato ketchup
1 tbls light soy sauce
300 ml (½ pint) dry white wine
2 tbls soft light brown sugar
a few herb sprigs

Wipe the chicken with absorbent kitchen paper and, using a sharp knife, score the flesh in 2 or 3 places. Place the chicken, cut side down, in a single layer in a shallow dish.

Combine the marinade ingredients and pour over the chicken. Turn to coat, cover and leave to marinate in the refrigerator for 8-12 hours, basting occasionally.

Heat the oven to 190°C, 375°F, Gas Mark 5. Remove the chicken, reserving the marinade. Season the chicken with salt and pepper and place in an oiled ovenproof dish.

Add the oil to the marinade, then spoon over the meat and cook in the oven for 35 minutes, basting several times.

Transfer to the barbecue and cook for a further 10 minutes, turning once, or until brown and tender.

Serve garnished with herb sprigs.

Serving idea: Serve with Baked corn on the cob (see page 34).
Variation: Use 4 large pork chops instead of the chicken pieces.

Parmesan chicken drumsticks

SERVES 4

25 g (1 oz) fresh white breadcrumbs
25 g (1 oz) Parmesan cheese, grated
1 tbls plain flour
salt and pepper
4 large chicken drumsticks, skinned
1 egg, beaten

Mix together the breadcrumbs and Parmesan cheese. Season the flour with salt and pepper. Coat the chicken drumsticks with seasoned flour, dip in the egg, then roll in the breadcrumb mixture, pressing it on with the fingertips. Make sure the pieces are thoroughly coated, then chill in the refrigerator for 30 minutes.

Cook on a hot barbecue for 30-40 minutes, turning frequently, until tender and cooked through.

Serving idea: Serve with Potato salad (see page 38) and a Spinach, bacon and mushroom salad (page 38).
Variation: Substitute 25 g (1 oz) finely chopped peanuts for the Parmesan.

Barbecued spare ribs

SERVES 4

1 kg (2 lb) pork spare ribs
1 tbls red wine vinegar
salt
fresh parsley, to garnish
For the sauce
2 tbls tomato ketchup
2 tbls clear honey
2 tbls soy sauce
2 tsp red wine vinegar
1/2 tsp English mustard powder
65 ml (2 1/2 fl oz) water
2 tsp Worcestershire sauce
1/2 tsp paprika
salt and pepper

Place the spare ribs and vinegar in a large saucepan of salted water. Bring to the boil, then simmer for 15 minutes.

Meanwhile, place all the sauce ingredients in a saucepan; stir well. Bring to the boil, then lower the heat and simmer for 5 minutes.

Strain the spare ribs, place in a large bowl and pour over the sauce. Leave until cool, turning frequently.

Remove the spare ribs, reserving the sauce. Cook the spare ribs on a hot barbecue, turning once, for 10-15 minutes, until crisp and brown.

Serve garnished with fresh parsley; reheat the sauce and hand round separately with the spare ribs.

Serving ideas: Serve with hot French bread and coleslaw.

Beef teriyaki

SERVES 4

4 tbls Japanese soy sauce
2 tbls dry sherry
2 tsp chopped fresh ginger root
1 garlic clove, crushed
4 rump or sirloin steaks, each
  weighing about 225 g (8 oz)
Dipping sauce
120 ml (4 fl oz) Japanese soy sauce
4 tbls dry sherry
3 spring onions, finely chopped
2 tsp chopped fresh ginger root
1 tsp lemon juice

Mix the soy sauce, sherry, ginger and garlic together in a shallow dish. Add the steaks and marinate at room temperature for 2 hours, turning occasionally.

Remove the steaks from the marinade using a slotted spoon. Reserve the marinade. Cook the meat over charcoal, about 15 cm (6 inches) above the fire. Turning and basting with the reserved marinade, cook for 3-4 minutes on each side for medium steaks or longer if you prefer well-done.

While the steaks are cooking, combine all the sauce ingredients and spoon into individual small bowls. Slice the cooked steaks into strips and serve with the dipping sauce.

● Parmesan chicken drumsticks; Barbecued spare ribs; Beef teriyaki

Baked corn on the cob

SERVES 4

4 corn cobs, husks and silk removed
sugar
salt
4 tbls water
50 g (2 oz) butter, melted, to serve

Place each corn cob on a piece of foil large enough to contain it and sprinkle with a little sugar, salt and 1 tbls water. Seal the edges of the foil firmly, to make parcels.

Cook on a hot barbecue for 20-30 minutes, or until tender. Open out the parcels and pour over the melted butter. Serve straight from the foil.

Serving ideas: Serve with barbecued chicken or lamb chops.
Variations: Other vegetables may be successfully cooked in foil on the barbecue. For baked courgettes, allow 1 courgette per person. Parboil for 4 minutes in salted water, then drain and cut into thick slices. Divide between 4 pieces of foil, adding a chopped tomato and seasoning to each before sealing.

Cream cheese stuffed potatoes

SERVES 4

4 large potatoes
salt and pepper
100 g (4 oz) full fat soft cheese
1 small onion, finely chopped
1 tbls snipped chives

Scrub the potatoes in cold water and pat dry with absorbent kitchen paper. Prick the skins all over with a fork and rub with salt.

Wrap each potato in foil and place amongst the hot coals of the barbecue. Bake for 40-50 minutes, turning frequently, or until the potatoes feel soft when pinched.

Meanwhile, cream together the cheese, onion and chives and season to taste with salt and pepper.

Scoop the flesh from the cooked potatoes and mix with the cream cheese mixture. Pile back into the potato shells and serve.

Serving ideas: Serve with a selection of barbecued meats and a mixed or leafy green salad.
Variation: Reduce the cooking time by parboiling the potatoes for 10 minutes before wrapping in foil.

● Baked corn on the cob; Cream cheese stuffed potatoes

Barbecue chilli beans

● Barbecue chilli beans; Red cabbage and pineapple coleslaw

SERVES 6

25g (1 oz) margarine or butter
1 large onion, chopped
4 rashers streaky bacon, rinded and
  chopped
¼ tsp chilli powder
198g (7 oz) can tomatoes
439g (15½oz) can baked beans
salt and pepper
dash of Worcestershire sauce

Melt the margarine in a saucepan, add the onion and fry gently for 5 minutes until soft and lightly coloured. Add the bacon to the pan and fry for about 8 minutes until crisp and golden.

Stir in the chilli powder, then the tomatoes with their juice and the baked beans. Stir well and simmer gently until heated through.

Season with salt, pepper and Worcestershire sauce to taste.

Serving ideas: Serve with barbecued sausages or beefburgers.

Red cabbage and pineapple coleslaw

SERVES 4

227 g (8 oz) can pineapple rings,
*   drained, syrup reserved*
6 spring onions, sliced
25 g (1 oz) sultanas
175 g (6 oz) red cabbage, shredded
2 tbls French dressing
salt and pepper
2 chopped spring onions, to garnish

Reserve 1 pineapple ring for the garnish.

Chop the remainder and place in a salad bowl with the spring onions, sultanas and cabbage.

Mix 1 tbls of the reserved pineapple syrup with the French dressing, season to taste with salt and pepper and add to the salad ingredients.

Toss well and serve garnished with the pineapple ring and chopped spring onions.

Serving ideas: Serve with barbecued pork chops or spare ribs.
Variation: Omit the spring onions and use 2 chopped celery stalks and 1 tbls coarsely chopped walnuts.

Spinach, bacon and mushroom salad

SERVES 4-6

4 rashers streaky bacon, rinded and
   chopped
225 g (8 oz) young spinach leaves
225 g (8 oz) button mushrooms, sliced
For the dressing
3 tbls olive oil
1 tbls lemon juice
1 garlic clove, crushed
1 tsp snipped chives
pinch of English mustard powder
salt and pepper

Place the bacon in a small frying pan
and heat gently until the fat runs. Fry
for a further 5 minutes, stirring from
time to time, or until crisp and golden.
Remove with a slotted spoon and drain
on absorbent kitchen paper. Leave to
cool.

Shred the spinach leaves, discarding
any tough stalks, and place in a salad
bowl. Add the bacon and mushrooms.

Place all the dressing ingredients in a
screw-top jar and shake until thoroughly mixed. Pour over the salad, toss
and serve immediately.

Serving ideas: Serve with barbecued
chicken or fish.
Variation: Fry small cubes of bread
with the bacon and add to the salad.

Potato salad

SERVES 4

450 g (1 lb) new potatoes
2 tsp olive oil
1 tsp white wine vinegar
4 tbls soured cream
salt and pepper
1 tbls snipped chives, to garnish

Cook the potatoes in boiling salted
water for 15-20 minutes, or until just
tender. Drain, and when cool enough
to handle cut into 1 cm (½ inch) pieces.
Place in a salad bowl.

Combine the oil and vinegar and
pour over the potatoes while still warm,
so that they absorb the dressing. Leave
to cool.

Whisk the soured cream with a fork,
then using a wooden spoon, carefully
mix it into the potatoes without breaking them up. Season with salt and pepper. Sprinkle with the chives before
serving.

Serving ideas: Serve with hamburgers
and barbecued chops and steaks.
Variation: Add 4 finely chopped
spring onions to the salad with the
soured cream.

Three bean salad

SERVES 4

100 g (4 oz) frozen green beans, cut
   into 1 cm (½ inch) pieces
salt
439 g (15½ oz) can butter beans,
   drained
439 g (15½ oz) can red kidney beans,
   drained
1 onion, chopped
3 tomatoes, quartered
For the dressing
4 tbls vegetable oil
2 tbls white wine vinegar
1 tsp French mustard
pinch of sugar
salt and pepper

Cook the green beans in boiling salted
water for 5 minutes. Drain; leave to
cool.

Place the green beans, butter beans,
kidney beans, onion and tomatoes in a
salad bowl and stir carefully to mix.

Place all the dressing ingredients in a
screw-top jar and shake until thoroughly mixed. Pour the dressing over
the beans and stir lightly until all the
ingredients are coated.

Serving ideas: Serve with barbecued
lamb or spare ribs.
Variation: Add ½ tsp cayenne pepper
to the dressing ingredients.

● Potato salad; Spinach, bacon and mushroom salad; Three bean salad

Greek salad

SERVES 4-6

1 Cos lettuce, shredded
½ cucumber, cut into chunks
225 g (8 oz) feta cheese, cut into cubes
4 tomatoes, skinned and sliced
6 anchovy fillets, finely chopped
6 large black olives, halved and
    stoned
large pinch of dried marjoram
1 tbls finely chopped fresh parsley
freshly ground black pepper
For the dressing
4 tbls olive oil
4 tsp white wine vinegar
1 tbls finely chopped fresh mixed
    herbs

4 spring onions, chopped
1 tsp sugar
salt and pepper

Place the shredded lettuce on a serving platter and arrange the cucumber, feta cheese, tomatoes, anchovies and olives on top. Sprinkle with the marjoram, parsley and plenty of black pepper.

Place all the dressing ingredients in a screw-top jar and shake well. Pour evenly over the salad and serve.

Serving ideas: Serve with kebabs or barbecued leg of lamb.
Variation: If feta cheese is not available, use Wensleydale, Lancashire, or Caerphilly instead.

Prawn, grape and cottage cheese salad

SERVES 4

1 head chicory
350 g (12 oz) cottage cheese
100 g (4 oz) green grapes, seeded
225 g (8 oz) peeled prawns
salt and pepper
4 tbls thick mayonnaise
4 tbls lemon juice
2 tbls finely chopped fresh parsley
lemon slices, to garnish

● Left: Greek salad; Right: Prawn, grape and cottage cheese salad

Separate the chicory leaves and use to line the base of a salad bowl. Mix the cottage cheese with the grapes and prawns and season to taste with salt and pepper. Carefully pile the mixture into the centre of the bowl over the chicory leaves.

Combine the mayonnaise, lemon juice and parsley and spoon evenly over the cottage cheese. Garnish with lemon slices.

Serving ideas: Serve the salad with cold ham or chicken, or on its own with wholemeal rolls and a bowl of chilled radishes.

Variation: Add ½ small melon cut into cubes or balls to the cottage cheese with the grapes.

BARBECUE DRINKS AND SWEETS

Sangria

SERVES 4

300 ml (½ pint) dry red wine
2 tbls brandy
65 ml (2½ fl oz) fresh orange juice,
* strained*
300 ml (½ pint) lemonade
For the decoration
½ orange, thinly sliced
½ lemon, thinly sliced
1 dessert apple, cored and thinly
* sliced*
ice cubes

Mix the red wine and brandy in a large
jug. Add the orange juice and lemonade
and stir well. Chill in the refrigerator for
2 hours.

Before serving, float the fruit slices
on top and add a few ice cubes.

Variations: If preferred omit the
brandy. Use cranberry juice instead of
orange juice for a delicious change.

Fresh lemonade

SERVES 4

8 tbls fresh lemon juice
ice cubes
soda water
For the sugar syrup
100 g (4 oz) sugar
300 ml (½ pint) water
To decorate
4 mint sprigs
4 lemon slices

To make the sugar syrup, place the
sugar and water in a saucepan and stir

over a low heat until dissolved. Leave
until cool.

Put 1 tbls of the sugar syrup in the
bottom of each of 4 tall glasses. Stir 2
tbls lemon juice into each glass and add
a few ice cubes.

Fill each glass with soda water and
decorate with mint and a lemon slice.

Variations: If a still drink is preferred
omit the soda water and fill the glasses
with ordinary water instead.

A variety of fruity drinks can be made
from this basic recipe by substituting
the following juices for the lemon juice:
orange, lime, pineapple, grapefruit.

Fruit punch

SERVES 4

150 ml (¼ pint) sugar syrup (see Fresh
* lemonade), cooled*
150 ml (¼ pint) orange juice, chilled
150 ml (¼ pint) pineapple juice,
* chilled*
300 ml (½ pint) weak cold tea,
* strained*
slices of fruit (such as orange, lemon,
* pineapple, apple)*
crushed ice
150 ml (¼ pint) ginger ale
mint sprigs, to decorate

Pour the sugar syrup into a jug and stir
in the fruit juices and the tea. Add the
fruit slices and the crushed ice. Mix
well. Pour into 4 tall glasses and top up
with ginger ale. Decorate each glass
with a mint sprig.

Variation: Use 150 ml (¼ pint) lemon
squash instead of the pineapple juice.

● Sangria; Fresh lemonade; Fruit punch

Baked pineapple slices

SERVES 4

*4 thick slices fresh pineapple, peeled
  and cored
4 tbls soft light brown sugar
2 tbls kirsch
mint sprigs, to decorate*

Place each pineapple slice in the centre
of a square of foil large enough to contain it. Sprinkle 1 tbls sugar over each
slice, then sprinkle the kirsch over the
top. Leave to stand for about 30 minutes, then seal the foil edges firmly to
make parcels.

Cook the pineapple parcels on a hot
barbecue for about 20 minutes, turning once, until the pineapple is tender.
Open the parcels and decorate with
mint sprigs.

Serving ideas: Serve with whipped
cream or scoops of ice cream.
Variation: Substitute grapefruit
halves for the pineapple.

Sweet rum sauce

Makes about 300 ml (½ pint)

*225 g (8 oz) caster sugar
300 ml (½ pint) water
4 tbls white rum
grated rind and juice of 1 orange*

Place the sugar and water in a saucepan and heat very gently, stirring from
time to time, until the sugar is dissolved. Add the rum and orange rind
and juice, bring to the boil and boil for
15 minutes.

Heat through on the barbecue when
required; use for dipping cubes of
baked fruit such as pineapple, or sliced
banana.

Variation: Use 4 tbls clear honey instead of half the sugar.

● Top row: Sweet rum sauce;
Blackcurrant sorbet; Bottom row:
Baked pineapple slices; Butterscotch ice
cream

Blackcurrant sorbet

SERVES 4

450g (1 lb) blackcurrants
2 tbls cassis
100g (4 oz) sugar
150ml (¼ pint) water
juice of ½ lemon
1 egg white

Simmer the blackcurrants in a pan with the cassis until soft, then purée in a blender or food processor.

Heat the sugar and water in a pan until dissolved. Raise the heat and boil for 5 minutes. Set aside to cool.

Add the cooled syrup to the black-currant purée with the lemon juice. Freeze in a rigid container for 2 to 3 hours.

Turn the blackcurrant mixture into a bowl; beat until mushy. Whip the egg white until stiff; fold into the mixture. Return to container; freeze until solid.

Transfer to the refrigerator 10 minutes before serving to soften.

Butterscotch ice cream

SERVES 4-6

100g (4 oz) soft dark brown sugar
150 ml (¼ pint) water
25g (1 oz) butter
2 tsp lemon juice
2 tsp arrowroot, blended with water
1 × 410g (14½ oz) can evaporated
  milk, chilled overnight
3 drops vanilla essence

Dissolve the sugar in the water over low heat. Add butter and lemon juice; cook rapidly, without stirring, 5 minutes.

Stir in arrowroot, reduce heat; simmer until thick. Set aside to cool.

Pour the evaporated milk into a bowl and, using a rotary beater, beat until thick and frothy. Fold in the cold butterscotch sauce and vanilla.

Pour the mixture into a freezer container and freeze. Beat twice, at hourly intervals. Cover, seal and freeze.

Curried prawn tartlets

MAKES 10

175 g (6 oz) plain flour
pinch of salt
40 g (1½ oz) lard
*40 g (1½ oz) block margarine or butter,
diced*
2-3 tbls cold water
For the filling
25 g (1 oz) margarine or butter
25 g (1 oz) plain flour
1 tsp curry paste or curry powder
300 ml (½ pint) milk
few drops anchovy essence
225 g (8 oz) peeled prawns
salt and pepper
To garnish
1 tsp paprika
10 parsley sprigs

Sift the flour with the salt into a mixing bowl, add the lard and margarine and rub in with the fingertips until the mixture resembles fine breadcrumbs. Using a round-bladed knife, mix in enough cold water to bind, then knead lightly on a floured work surface, wrap in cling film and chill in the refrigerator while preparing the filling.

Melt the margarine in a saucepan, then stir in the flour and curry paste over a low heat. Cook, stirring, for 2-3 minutes, then remove from the heat and gradually stir in the milk.

Return the saucepan to the heat and bring gently to simmering point, stirring constantly. Simmer for 4-5 minutes, then stir in the anchovy essence. Pour the sauce into a bowl, cover with cling film and leave to cool.

Meanwhile, heat the oven to 190°C, 375°F, Gas Mark 5. Roll out the pastry on a floured surface and cut into 10 rounds, using a 7.5 cm (3 inch) fluted pastry cutter.

Press the rounds into tartlet tins, prick the bases with a fork and bake in the oven for 15-20 minutes until crisp and golden. Transfer the baked tartlet cases to a wire rack to cool completely.

When the curry sauce is cold, stir in the prawns (reserving 10 for garnish), with salt and pepper to taste. Fill the cold pastry cases with the mixture. Garnish each with a prawn, sprinkle over a little paprika, and add a parsley sprig.

Pack in a tin or polythene cake container.

Variation: Add 75 g (3 oz) grated Gruyère cheese to the sauce after stirring in the milk.

Potted chicken

SERVES 4-6

100 g (4 oz) butter
*1 onion, minced or very finely
chopped*
1-2 garlic cloves, crushed
*225 g (8 oz) boneless cooked chicken
meat, skin removed and finely
minced*
2 tbls medium sherry
about 4 tbls chicken stock
salt and pepper
pinch of grated nutmeg
pinch of dried mixed herbs
To garnish
stuffed olives
tomato slices

Melt half the butter in a frying pan, add the onion and garlic and fry gently for 5 minutes until soft and lightly coloured. Stir in the minced chicken followed by the sherry and enough stock just to moisten. Season to taste with salt, pepper and nutmeg, and stir in the herbs.

Press the chicken mixture into 4 greased individual ramekins and level the tops. Chill in the refrigerator until firm.

Melt the remaining butter and pour a thin layer over each ramekin. Chill in the refrigerator for 2-3 days until required.

Serve garnished with thin slices of the stuffed olives and slices of tomato. Transport to the picnic in the ramekins, covered with foil.

Serving ideas: Serve with slices of brown bread and butter and cold gherkins or radishes.

Variation: Use other cooked meats such as beef, turkey or ham instead of the chicken.

● Top: Potted chicken;
Bottom: Curried prawn tartlets

Chilled tomato and orange soup

SERVES 4-6

25 g (1 oz) margarine or butter
100 g (4 oz) red lentils
1 carrot, chopped
1 large onion, chopped
thinly pared rind and juice of 1 orange
750 g (1½ lb) tomatoes, skinned and
    chopped
1 bay leaf
900 ml (1½ pints) chicken stock
salt and pepper
1 tbls snipped chives, to garnish

Melt the margarine in a large saucepan. Add the lentils, carrot and onion and fry over a gentle heat for about 5 minutes until softened, stirring occasionally.

Add the orange rind to the pan with the tomatoes and bay leaf. Pour in the stock, season to taste, then bring to the boil. Cover and simmer for 1 hour, or until all the ingredients are soft.

Discard the bay leaf, then purée the soup in a liquidizer or press through a sieve. Stir in the orange juice and adjust the seasoning to taste.

Chill the soup for at least 2 hours. Stir in a little extra cold chicken stock if it is too thick, adjust the seasoning to taste and garnish with chives. Transport in an insulated jug or thermos flask.

Serving idea: Serve with French bread.
Variation: Omit the lentils and use a diced potato instead.

● Chilled tomato and orange soup; Cream of mushroom soup

Cream of mushroom soup

SERVES 4

15 g (¹/₂ oz) margarine or butter
1 small onion, finely chopped
225 g (8 oz) mushrooms, finely
    chopped
1¹/₂ tbls plain flour
900 ml (1¹/₂ pints) chicken stock
salt and pepper
pinch of grated nutmeg
1 bay leaf
150 ml (¹/₄ pint) single cream
1 tbls chopped fresh parsley, to
    garnish

Melt the margarine in a large saucepan. Add the onion and mushrooms, cover and cook gently for 5 minutes until soft. Stir in the flour and cook for a further 2 minutes, stirring constantly.

Gradually add the chicken stock and bring to the boil. Season to taste, add the nutmeg and bay leaf, lower the heat, half cover and simmer gently for about 20 minutes.

Remove from the heat, discard the bay leaf; stir in the cream. Garnish with parsley. Transport in a vacuum flask.

Serving idea: Serve with crusty wholemeal bread.
Variation: Serve this soup chilled with a garnish of chives instead of parsley.

49

Raised picnic pie

SERVES 4

450 g (1 lb) plain flour
1 tsp salt
100 g (4 oz) lard
150 ml (¼ pint) water
4 tbls milk
beaten egg or milk, to glaze
15 g (½ oz) sachet powdered gelatine
150 ml (¼ pint) chicken stock
For the filling
450 g (1 lb) boneless cooked chicken,
*   skin removed and chopped*
225 g (8 oz) cooked ham or bacon,
*   chopped*
1 small onion, finely chopped
salt and pepper
½ tsp dried thyme
225 g (8 oz) sausagemeat

Heat the oven to 200°C, 400°F, Gas Mark 6. Grease a game pie mould or 18 cm (7 inch) loose-bottomed round cake tin.

To make the pastry, sift the flour with the salt into a mixing bowl. Place the lard in a saucepan with the water and milk. Heat gently until the lard melts, then bring to the boil.

Pour all at once into the flour and mix to form a pliable dough, then knead lightly. Remove three-quarters of the dough to a lightly floured surface, keeping the remainder warm in the bowl covered with a cloth. Roll out the dough and use to line the greased pie mould or cake tin.

To make the filling, mix together the chicken, ham and onion and season with salt, pepper and the thyme. Spread the sausagemeat in a thin layer in the mould or tin, then spoon in the chicken mixture.

Roll out the reserved dough for the lid, dampen the edges and position over the pie. Press the edges together firmly, then trim and crimp. Roll out the trimmings and use to make leaves. Make a hole in the centre of the pie lid and decorate with dough leaves. Brush the top with beaten egg or milk.

Bake the pie in the oven for 30 minutes. Reduce the temperature to 160°C, 325°F, Gas Mark 3 and bake for a further 1-1½ hours, until the pastry is golden brown. Cover with grease-proof paper if the pastry shows signs of overbrowning. Cool on a wire rack, then carefully unmould.

Dissolve the gelatine in the stock in a heatproof basin set over a pan of hot water. Pour through the hole in the centre of the pie. Chill the pie in the

refrigerator overnight before serving.

Transport wrapped in a double thickness of foil.

Serving idea: Serve with crisp lettuce and tomatoes.
Variation: Spoon half the chicken mixture over the sausagemeat, then press in 2 hard-boiled eggs. Cover with the remaining chicken mixture.

Picnic meat loaf

SERVES 4

225 g (8 oz) minced beef
350 g (12 oz) minced pork
4 tbls thyme and parsley stuffing mix
1 tbls Worcestershire sauce
1 tbls tomato ketchup
1 onion, finely chopped
1 garlic clove, crushed
salt and pepper
1 egg, beaten

Heat the oven to 180°C, 350°F, Gas Mark 4. Grease a 1 kg (2 lb) loaf tin.

Place all the ingredients except the egg in a large bowl and stir well to mix.

Stir the beaten egg into the mixture to bind, then spoon into the greased tin. Cover with foil and bake in the oven for 1 hour, until firm.

Remove from the oven and leave to stand for 5 minutes, then pour off the excess fat and leave until cold. Transport to the picnic wrapped in double thickness foil.

Serving ideas: Serve with Russian salad (see page 56) and sliced tomatoes and cucumbers.
Variation: Instead of the stuffing mix use 50 g (2 oz) fresh wholemeal breadcrumbs with 1 tbls chopped fresh herbs.

● Left: Raised picnic pie;
Right: Picnic meat loaf

Cheese and onion tarts

SERVES 4

100 g (4 oz) plain flour
pinch of salt
25 g (1 oz) block margarine or butter,
*   diced*
25 g (1 oz) lard, diced
1-2 tbls water
For the filling
15 g (½ oz) margarine or butter
1 onion, chopped
1 dessert apple, peeled, cored and
*   grated*
50 g (2 oz) mature Cheddar cheese,
*   grated*
1 egg
about 100 ml (3½ fl oz) milk
salt and pepper

Heat the oven to 190°C, 375°F, Gas Mark 5.

To make the pastry, sift the flour with the salt into a mixing bowl. Add the margarine and lard and rub in with the fingertips until the mixture resembles fine breadcrumbs. Using a round-bladed knife, mix in enough water to make a firm dough.

● Cheese and onion tarts; Chicken and asparagus pasties

Divide the dough into 4 equal portions. Roll each portion out on a floured board or work surface and use to line four 10 cm (4 inch) tart tins or Yorkshire pudding tins.

To make the filling, melt the margarine in a small frying pan, add the onion and fry gently for 5 minutes until soft and lightly coloured. Divide the onion equally among the pastry cases and cover with the apple and cheese.

Beat the egg in a measuring jug and make up to 150 ml (¼ pint) with milk. Season and pour into the pastry cases.

Bake the tarts in the oven for 30-35 minutes or until the filling is set and golden. Remove from the oven and leave to cool for a few minutes in the tins, then transfer to a wire rack to cool completely.

Transport the tarts individually wrapped in double thickness foil.

Serving idea: Serve with celery stalks.
Variation: Use 2 slices cooked ham, chopped, instead of the apple.

Chicken and asparagus pasties

SERVES 4

225 g (8 oz) self-raising flour
1 tsp salt
50 g (2 oz) lard, diced
50 g (2 oz) block margarine or butter, diced
3-4 tbls water
beaten egg, to glaze
For the filling
198 g (7 oz) can asparagus tips, drained and chopped, liquid reserved
milk
15 g (½ oz) margarine or butter
1 tbls plain flour
225 g (8 oz) boneless cooked chicken, skin removed and finely chopped
salt and pepper

Heat the oven to 200°C, 400°F, Gas Mark 6. To make the pastry, sift the flour with the salt into a mixing bowl. Add the lard and margarine and rub in with the fingertips until the mixture resembles fine breadcrumbs. Using a round-bladed knife, mix in enough water to make a firm dough. Wrap in cling film and chill in the refrigerator while making the filling.

Make the asparagus liquid up to 150 ml (¼ pint) with milk.

Melt the margarine in a saucepan, stir in the flour and cook over a low heat for 1 minute. Gradually stir in the liquid mixture and bring to the boil, stirring constantly until thickened and smooth. Remove from the heat and add the chicken, chopped asparagus and salt and pepper to taste. Leave until completely cool.

Roll out the dough on a floured surface and cut four 18 cm (7 inch) rounds, using a small plate as a guide. Spoon a portion of filling into the centre of each round, dampen the edges, form into a semi-circle and seal the edges firmly. Flute the edges or decorate with the prongs of a fork.

Brush the pasties with beaten egg, place on a baking sheet and bake in the oven for about 30 minutes until golden brown. Transfer to a wire rack and leave to cool completely. Transport the pasties wrapped individually in double thickness foil.

Cold devilled chicken

SERVES 4

1.5 kg (3½ lb) chicken
2 carrots, chopped
1 celery stalk, chopped
1 bouquet garni
6 whole black peppercorns
½ tsp salt
2 tbls melted butter
1 tbls chopped fresh parsley, to garnish
For the sauce
3 tbls Worcestershire sauce
2 tbls red wine vinegar
1 spring onion, finely chopped
1 tbls lemon juice
1 garlic clove, crushed
½ × 198 g (7 oz) can tomatoes, drained and chopped
salt and pepper
1 bay leaf

Place the chicken in a large saucepan and arrange the carrots, celery and bouquet garni around it. Add the peppercorns and salt and pour in enough fresh cold water to cover the chicken. Bring to the boil over high heat.

Reduce the heat to low, cover and simmer gently for 1-1¼ hours, or until the chicken is tender and the juices run clear when pierced in the thickest part with the point of a sharp knife. Remove from the heat and leave the chicken to cool in the stock.

When the chicken is cold, remove it from the stock. Strain the stock into a jug and reserve 300 ml (½ pint).

Heat the grill to moderate. Skin the chicken and cut into eight serving pieces. Place in a large shallow casserole and brush with melted butter.

Grill for about 5 minutes on each side or until all the pieces are lightly browned. Set aside.

To make the sauce, place all the ingredients in a saucepan and bring gradually to the boil. Reduce the heat, then simmer for 10 minutes. Discard the bay leaf and pour the sauce over the chicken.

Leave until cold. Before serving, garnish with chopped parsley. Transport in the casserole.

Serving idea: Serve with Rice salad (see page 59) and a green salad.
Variation: Instead of a whole chicken, use 4 chicken quarters. Simmer for about 30 minutes or until tender.

Spinach quiche

SERVES 4

150 g (6 oz) plain wholemeal flour
pinch of salt
75 g (3 oz) block margarine or butter, diced
2-3 tbls water
25 g (1 oz) Parmesan cheese, grated
For the filling
450 g (1 lb) spinach
50 g (2 oz) Cheddar cheese, grated
142 ml (5 fl oz) carton single cream
2 eggs
½ tsp grated nutmeg
salt and pepper

Heat the oven to 190°C, 375°F, Gas Mark 5. To make the pastry, sift the flour with the salt into a mixing bowl and tip in the bran from the sieve. Add the margarine and rub in with the fingertips until the mixture resembles fine breadcrumbs. Using a round-bladed knife, mix in enough water to make a firm dough.

Turn the dough on to a floured board or work surface and knead lightly. Roll out and use to line a 20 cm (8 inch) flan tin. Chill in the refrigerator while preparing the filling.

Thoroughly wash the spinach, discarding the stalks and any tough leaves. Place in a saucepan, cover and simmer over moderate heat, with no added water, for about 5 minutes or until tender. Drain and chop finely.

● Top: Spinach quiche; Bottom: Cold devilled chicken

Place the chopped spinach in a large bowl and add the remaining filling ingredients. Beat well until throughly blended and pour into the chilled flan case.

Sprinkle the Parmesan cheese over the top and bake the quiche in the oven for 35 minutes or until firm and golden. Remove from the oven and leave until cold. Transport to the picnic carefully wrapped in foil or cling film.

Serving idea: Serve with a Three bean salad (see page 38).

Variation: Sprinkle the pastry base with 4 rashers streaky bacon, lightly fried and chopped, before adding the spinach filling.

Russian salad

SERVES 4-6

*450 g (1 lb) potatoes, cooked and
    diced
100 g (4 oz) carrots, cooked and sliced
100 g (4 oz) peas, cooked
2 celery stalks, finely chopped
2 gherkins, chopped
a few capers, to garnish*
For the dressing
*2 tbls vegetable oil
1 tbls white wine vinegar
pinch of sugar
salt and pepper
150 ml (¼ pint) thick mayonnaise*

Place the potatoes in a bowl. Add the
carrots, peas, celery and gherkins and
stir well to mix.

Place the oil, vinegar, sugar, salt and
pepper in a screw-top jar and shake
well. Pour over the vegetables and toss
thoroughly, then gently mix in the
mayonnaise.

Sprinkle the salad with the capers
before serving. Transport in a rigid lidded container.

Serving ideas: Serve with any cold
meats such as roast beef, pork or ham.
Variation: Add 1 small cooked chopped
beetroot to the other salad ingredients.

Courgette, pepper and tomato salad

SERVES 4-6

*450 g (1 lb) small courgettes, trimmed
    and sliced
225 g (8 oz) tomatoes, skinned and
    quartered
1 red pepper, cored, seeded and diced
1 green pepper, cored, seeded and
    diced
a few black olives, stoned, to garnish*
For the dressing
*3 tbls vegetable oil
2 tbls lemon juice
salt and pepper
2 tsp dried oregano*

Place the courgettes in a saucepan of
lightly salted water. Bring to the boil,
cook for 2-3 minutes, then strain and
plunge into cold water. Drain again.

Place the courgettes in a large bowl
with the tomatoes and peppers.

Place all the dressing ingredients in a
screw-top jar and shake until thoroughly mixed. Pour over the vegetables
and toss lightly. Garnish with black
olives before serving. Transport in a
rigid container.

Wholemeal Scotch eggs

SERVES 4

5 eggs
25 g (1 oz) plain flour
salt and pepper
225 g (8 oz) pork sausagemeat
50 g (2 oz) wholemeal breadcrumbs,
   toasted, for coating
vegetable oil, for deep frying

Hard-boil 4 of the eggs. Drain, plunge into cold water and leave to cool, then shell. Season the flour with salt and pepper and use to coat the hard-boiled eggs.

Divide the sausagemeat into 4 equal portions and on a floured board or work surface roll each piece into a circle large enough to cover an egg completely.

Place 1 egg in the centre of each sausagemeat circle and carefully mould the sausagemeat round the egg. Pinch the edges together firmly, to seal.

Beat the remaining egg and use to coat the Scotch eggs, then roll in the breadcrumbs, until thoroughly coated.

Heat the oil in a deep fat fryer to 170°C, 340°F, or until a stale bread cube browns in 60 seconds, and deep fry the Scotch eggs for about 8 minutes until crisp and lightly browned. Drain on absorbent paper and leave to cool. Transport wrapped individually in foil or cling film, in a rigid container.

Serving ideas: Serve with Potato salad (see page 38), tomatoes and mustard.
Variation: Add ½ tsp dried sage to the sausagemeat.

● **Russian salad; Wholemeal Scotch eggs; Courgette, pepper and tomato salad**

● Cucumber and mint salad; Rice salad; Curried pasta salad

Cucumber and mint salad

SERVES 4

½ large cucumber, unpeeled and
  diced
salt
grated rind and juice of 1 lemon
1 garlic clove, crushed
2 tsp caster sugar
6 tbls olive oil
4 spring onions, chopped
2 tbls chopped fresh mint
pepper
a few mint leaves, to garnish

Place the cucumber in a colander set over a plate. Sprinkle with salt and leave for 20 minutes to drain, then rinse and drain on absorbent kitchen paper.

Meanwhile, combine the lemon rind and juice, garlic, sugar, oil, spring onions, chopped mint and pepper.

Place the drained cucumber in a rigid lidded bowl and spoon over the mint and lemon dressing. Garnish with mint leaves before serving.

Serving idea: Serve as a refreshing accompaniment to any barbecued lamb or fish.
Variation: Use only 1 tbls olive oil in the dressing and add a 150 g (5.29 oz) carton natural yoghurt to the other dressing ingredients.

Curried pasta salad

SERVES 4

225 g (8 oz) pasta shapes
1 small onion, finely chopped
4 tbls dry white vermouth
150 ml (¼ pint) mayonnaise
2 tsp mild curry paste
2 tsp apricot jam
2 tsp lemon juice
4 large sausages, cooked and thinly
  sliced
To garnish
2 tomatoes, sliced
a few black olives, stoned

Cook the pasta in a saucepan of boiling salted water for 12-15 minutes or until just tender. Drain well and leave to cool.

Place the onion and vermouth in a saucepan and bring to the boil. Simmer for 3 minutes. Remove from the heat and leave to cool.

Stir the mayonnaise, curry paste, apricot jam and lemon juice into the onion mixture. Pour over the pasta; toss to coat evenly. Fold in sausage.

Turn the mixture into a rigid lidded bowl. Garnish with the tomato slices and black olives before serving.

Serving ideas: Serve as a main dish with a green salad and French bread.

Rice salad

SERVES 4

225 g (8 oz) long-grain rice
12 whole cardamom pods
salt
227 g (8 oz) can pineapple rings,
  drained and roughly chopped
½ cucumber, peeled and diced
50 g (2 oz) hazelnuts, roasted and
  skinned
a little paprika, to finish
For the dressing
finely grated rind and juice of 1 orange
6 tbls vegetable oil
2 tsp curry paste

Cook the rice with the cardamom pods in a saucepan of boiling salted water for 10-15 minutes or until the rice is just tender. Drain the rice and rinse in cold water. Remove the cardamom pods and place the rice in a rigid polythene lidded bowl.

Add the chopped pineapple, cucumber and hazelnuts; stir well to mix.

Place all the dressing ingredients in a screw-top jar and shake to mix thoroughly. Pour the dressing over the rice salad and fork through evenly. Sprinkle a little paprika over the top.

Serving ideas: Serve with cold chicken or ham.

Layered sandwich loaf

SERVES 4-6

18 cm (7 inch) round granary or
wholemeal loaf
butter, softened for spreading
Egg filling
3 eggs, beaten
1 tbls milk
15 g (½ oz) butter
salt and pepper
3 spring onions, finely chopped
Chicken filling
175 g (6 oz) cooked chicken, minced
1 celery stalk, thinly sliced
2-3 tbls thick mayonnaise
1 tsp curry paste
Cheese filling
175 g (6 oz) Cheddar cheese, finely
grated
2 tomatoes, skinned and finely
chopped

First make the fillings. Put the eggs into
a non-stick saucepan with the milk,
butter and salt and pepper. Cook over a
gentle heat, stirring, until scrambled
but still creamy. Remove from the heat,
add the spring onions and leave to cool.

Combine the chicken and celery in a
bowl. Stir in enough mayonnaise to
give a spreading consistency and add
curry paste to taste. Stir well to mix.

Mix the cheese with the tomato.

Cut the loaf horizontally into 4 layers.
Spread each cut surface with butter.
Spread a layer with each filling and
reassemble the loaf. Wrap in foil until
required.

To serve, unwrap and slice vertically.

Variations: Vary the filling layers
according to taste – try egg and ham
mayonnaise, tuna and onion, minced
pork with apple and salad cream, or
garlic sausage with spring onion tops.

Cheese 'n' salami loaf

SERVES 4

1 small French loaf
butter, softened for spreading
100 g (4 oz) Cheddar cheese, sliced
2 tomatoes, sliced
50 g (2 oz) salami, rinded and sliced

Make diagonal cuts in the loaf at regu-
lar intervals; do not cut through the
bottom crust. Spread the cut surfaces
with butter; place the cheese, tomato
and salami between each bread slice.

Wrap in foil. To serve, unwrap and
cut between the bread slices.

Variation: Heat the loaf on a barbecue
until the cheese has melted.

Double decker baps

1-2 BAPS PER PERSON

butter, softened for spreading
2 fillings (see below)

Cut each bap horizontally into 3 layers.
Spread the cut surfaces with butter,
use two different fillings to sandwich
the layers and reassemble the baps.

Filling suggestions
1. *bottom layer: chopped cooked
chicken and chutney*
top layer: sliced chicory and tomato
2. *bottom layer: mashed sardine with
tomato slices*
*top layer: avocado mashed with a
little lemon juice*
3. *bottom layer: cold scrambled egg
and chives*
*top layer: chopped watercress and
walnuts*

● Double decker baps; Layered sandwich loaf; Cheese 'n' salami loaf

Sandwiches

Provide a variety of sandwiches by offering not only a choice of fillings but also a number of different breads.

Below are different types of bread with appropriate filling suggestions.

White bread sandwiches: sliced beef with horseradish; grated Cheddar cheese with raisins and mayonnaise

Wholemeal sandwiches or rolls: chopped peeled prawns with cottage cheese and lemon juice; cooked kipper fillets with butter and lemon juice.

Finger rolls: chopped turkey with cranberry sauce and lettuce

White crusty rolls: crumbled crispy bacon with mashed banana.

Rye bread sandwiches: cream cheese with sliced raw mushrooms; tongue with mustard and sliced gherkin

Sesame buns: grated blue cheese with chopped walnuts and lettuce

Pinwheel sandwiches

MAKES 30 SANDWICHES

156 g (5¹/₂ oz) can smooth liver pâté
50 g (2 oz) full fat soft cheese
1 tsp lemon juice
1 tbls snipped chives
5 slices of bread from a sandwich loaf,
  crusts removed

Beat together the pâté, soft cheese, lemon juice and chives. Spread over one side of each slice of bread. Roll the bread up carefully from one short end, like a Swiss roll. Cut each roll across into six slices.

Serving idea: These little sandwiches are suitable for children's picnics.
Variation: Vary the filling – for adults, use cod's roe pâté instead of liver pâté, or for a special occasion use thin slices of smoked salmon sprinkled with lemon juice and black pepper.

• Sandwiches; Pitta pockets; Pinwheel sandwiches

Pitta pockets

1 PIECE OF PITTA BREAD PER PERSON
FILLING (SEE BELOW)

Heat the oven to 150°C, 300°F, Gas Mark 2. Place the pitta bread on a baking sheet and heat through for about 10 minutes.

Cut each piece of pitta bread in half crossways. Carefully prise open the pitta bread along the cut edge and spoon the chosen filling into the opening.

Wrap in foil and either pack in an insulated bag to keep warm or eat cold.

Suggested fillings (quantities for 4)
1. Sausage and coleslaw: slice 4 cooked sausages and mix with ½ small white cabbage, shredded, 150 ml (¼ pint) mayonnaise, salt, pepper and 1 tbls chopped fresh parsley.

2. Lamb: mix 450 g (1 lb) cooked chopped or minced lamb with 2 chopped celery stalks, 2 tomatoes, skinned and chopped, 100 g (4 oz) cooked rice, 6 dried apricots, chopped, and 1 tbls chopped fresh coriander or parsley.
3. Curried beef: mix 450 g (1 lb) cooked chopped or minced beef with 1 grated eating apple, 2 tbls sultanas, 1 tbls curry paste and 142 ml (5 fl oz) carton soured cream.
4. Spicy peas and potatoes: heat 3 tbls of oil in a saucepan and add 1 tsp black mustard seeds. Cover and when the seeds stop spluttering add 1 tsp turmeric and 1 chopped green chilli. Stir and immediately add 450 g (1 lb) boiled cubed potatoes and 275 g (10 oz) cooked peas. Stir well to mix. Add salt to taste and the juice of ½ lemon. Taste the mixture and add more seasoning if necessary.

63

INDEX

Note: this includes variations supplied in recipes as well as the main recipes.